D0426521

My Dear Children

Mother Teresa's Last Message

by Mother Teresa

edited by

Hiroshi Katayanagi, S.J.

Paulist Press

New York/Mahwah, N.J.

First published by Don Bosco Press, Tokyo, Japan.

Caseside design by Cynthia Dunne
Interior design by Lynn Else

Copyright © 2001 Hiroshi Katayanagi, S.J.
English translation by Hiroshi Katayanagi

All rights reserved. No part of this book may be reproduced or transmitted in any form or by any means, electronic or mechanical, including photocopying, recording or by any information storage and retrieval system without permission from the Publisher.

Library of Congress Cataloging-in-Publication Data

Katayanagi, Hiroshi.
    My dear children : Mother Teresa's last message / by Mother Teresa; edited by Hiroshi Katayanagi.
       p. cm.
    Includes bibliographical references.
    ISBN 0-8091-0553-5
    1. Teresa, Mother, 1910—Pictorial works. 2. Missionaries of Charity—Pictorial works. 3. Nuns—India—Calcutta—Biography—Pictorial works. I. Title.
    BX4406.5.Z8 K38 2002
    271'.97—dc21

2002006694

This edition published by Paulist Press
997 Macarthur Boulevard
Mahwah, New Jersey 07430

www.paulistpress.com

Printed and bound in the United States of America

Contents

Preface by Lawrence Boadt, C.S.P. / v

Favorite Prayers / 3

A Letter from Varanasi / 7

Diary of Mother's Early Days / 20

A Speech / 24

An Interview / 37

Letters from Mother's Last Years / 41

The Last Letter / 55

Afterword / 62

Sources and Notes / 66

Picture Captions / 68

Preface

Over the years, I have listened to the stories of perhaps two dozen men and women who have journeyed to the convent of the Sisters of Charity in Calcutta to spend time living, praying and working with Mother Teresa and her community. All of them recount how deeply moved they were by the experience, but many also note how startled they were to discover it wasn't what they had expected. Mother Teresa was not a plaster saint, serene and gliding through the day lost in prayer; she was a vibrant woman of action and concern, laboring side by side with her sisters, and often sharing her thoughts as she tended the dying or worked on more mundane administrative tasks. Perhaps many thought a Nobel Peace Prize winner would be more aloof or pre-occupied with world events, but instead those who met her went away impressed most of all by the simple and direct words she spoke to them and to those she served.

This small book of photos comes from just two years before Mother Teresa died. The words come mostly from her last years. Together, they are a brief but enduring snapshot into the daily life of the Sisters of Charity and their foundress, but perhaps all the more powerful because these pages capture not the most unique or important or powerful words she ever spoke, but the typical *daily* expression of her love of God reflected in and for others. It is a tribute to the same spirit of God's service to others that has led Hiroshi Katayanagi, S.J., to share them with us.

Lawrence Boadt, C.S.P.
Publisher

My Dear Children

Mother Teresa's Last Message

Favorite Prayers

"I will, I want, with

God's blessing, to be holy."

"You did it to me."

Mary, mother of Jesus, give me your heart,

so beautiful, so pure, so immaculate, so full of

love and humility that I may be able to receive

Jesus in the Bread of Life, love Him as you

loved Him, serve Him in the distressing

disguise of the Poorest of the Poor.

A Letter from Varanasi

I worry some of you still have not really met Jesus—one to one—you and Jesus alone. We may spend time in chapel—but have you seen with the eyes of your soul how He looks at you with love? Do you really know the living Jesus—not from books but from being with Him in your heart? Have you heard the loving words He speaks to you? Ask for the grace; He is longing to give it.

Until you can hear Jesus in the silence of your own heart, you will not be able to hear Him saying "I thirst" in the hearts of the poor. Never give up this daily intimate contact with Jesus as the real living person—not just the idea. How can we last even one day without hearing Jesus say "I love you"—impossible. Our soul needs that as much as the body needs to breathe the air. If not, prayer is dead—meditation only thinking. Jesus wants you each to hear Him—speaking in the silence of your heart.

Be careful of all that can block that personal contact with the living Jesus. The Devil may try to use the hurts of life and sometimes your own mistakes to make you feel it is impossible that Jesus really loves you, is really cleaving to you. This is a danger for all of us. And so sad, because it is completely opposite of what Jesus is really wanting, waiting to tell you.

Not only that He loves you, but even more—He thirsts for you. Not only that He loves you, but even more—He longs for you. He misses you when you don't come close. He thirsts for you. He loves you always, even when you don't feel worthy. When not accepted by others, even by yourself sometimes—He is the one who always accepts you. My children, you don't have to be different for Jesus to love you. Only believe you are precious to Him. Bring all you are suffering to His feet—only open your heart to be loved by Him as you are. He will do the rest.

Why does Jesus say "I thirst"? What does it mean? Something so hard to explain in words—if you remember anything from Mother's letter, remember this— "I thirst" is something much deeper than just Jesus saying "I love you." Until you know deep inside that Jesus thirsts for you, you can't begin to know who He wants to be for you. Or who He wants you to be for Him.

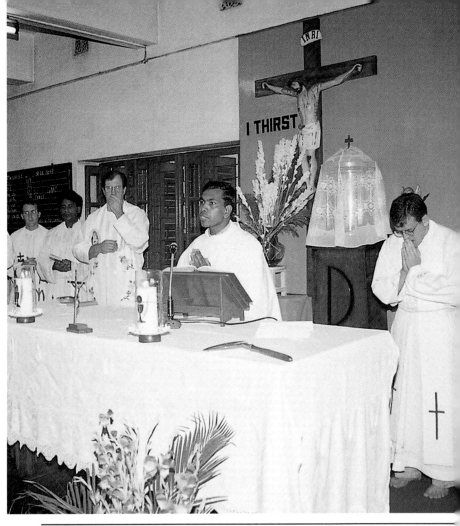

Ask yourself, would it make any difference in my vocation, in my relation to Jesus, in my work if Jesus' thirst were no longer our Aim— no longer on the chapel wall? Would anything change in my life? Would I feel any loss? Ask yourself honestly, and let this be a test for each to see if His thirst is a reality, something alive—not just an idea.

"I thirst" and "You did it to me"—remember always to connect the two, the means with the aim. What God has joined together let no one split apart. Do not underestimate our practical means—the work for the poor, no matter how small or humble—that makes our life something beautiful for God.

How do you approach the thirst of Jesus? Only one secret—

the closer you come to Jesus, the better you will know His thirst. "Repent and believe," Jesus tells us. What are we to repent? Our indifference, our hardness of heart. What are we to believe? Jesus thirsts even now, in your heart and in the poor—He knows your weakness, He wants only your love, wants only the chance to love you. He is not bound by time. Whenever we come close to Him—we become partners of Our Lady, St. John, Magdalen. Hear Him. Hear your own name. Make my joy and yours complete.

Diary of Mother's Early Days

Today I learned a good lesson—the poverty of the poor must often be so hard for them. When I went round looking for a home, I walked and walked till my legs and arms ached. I thought how they must also ache in body and soul looking for home, food, help. Then the temptation grew strong. The palace buildings of Loreto came rushing into my mind. All the beautiful things and comforts— in a word everything. "You have only to say a word and all that will be yours again," the tempter kept on saying. Of free choice, my God, and out of love for you, I desire to remain and do whatever be Your holy will. This is the dark night of the birth of the Society. My God give me courage now, this moment, to persevere in following your will.

Today my God, what tortures of loneliness. I wonder how long my heart will suffer this. Tears roll and roll. Everyone sees my weakness. My God, give me courage now to fight self and the tempter. Let me not draw back from the sacrifice I have made of my free choice and conviction. Immaculate Heart of my Mother, have pity on thy poor child. For love of thee I want to live and die a Missionary of Charity.

A Speech

As if that was not enough—it was not enough

to become a man—He died on the cross to

*show that greater love, and He died for you
and for me and for the leper and for that man
dying of hunger and that naked person lying in
the street not only of Calcutta, but of Africa
and New York and London and Oslo—and
insisted that we love one another as He loves
each one of us. And we read that in the
Gospel very clearly: "...love as I have loved
you; as I love you; as the Father has loved me,
I love you."*

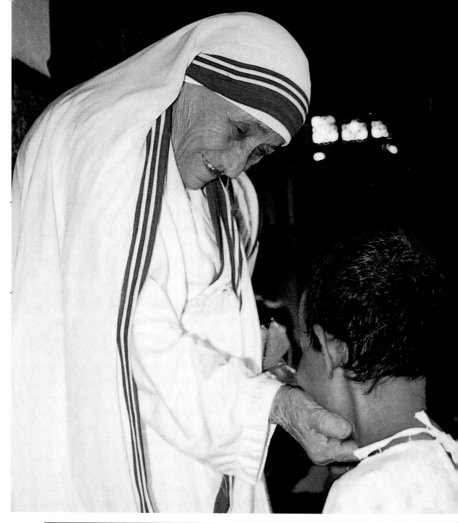

It is not enough for us to say: "I love God,

but I do not love my neighbor." St. John says

that you are a liar if you say you love God and

you don't love your neighbor. How can you love

God whom you do not see, if you do not love

your neighbor whom you see, whom you touch,

with whom you live? And this is very important

for us to realize that love, to be true,

has to hurt.

I went there (a home for old people), and I saw in that home they had everything, beautiful things, but everybody was looking toward the door. And I did not see a single one with a smile on their face. And I turned to the sister and I asked: How is that? How is it that these people who have everything here, why are they all looking toward the door? Why are they not smiling?

I am used to seeing the smiles on our people, even the dying ones smile. And she said: "This is nearly every day. They are expecting, they are hoping that a son or daughter will come to visit them. They are hurt because they are forgotten." And see—this is where love comes. That poverty comes right there in our own home, even neglect to love. Maybe in our own family we have somebody who is feeling lonely, who is feeling sick, who is feeling worried, and these are difficult days for everybody. Are we there? Are we there to receive them?

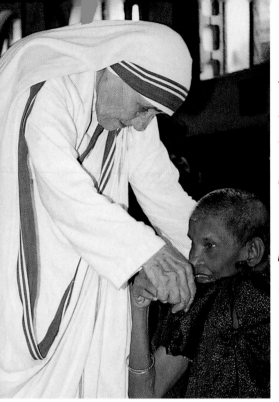

I believe that we are not really social workers. We may be doing social work in the eyes of the people, but we are really contemplatives in the heart of the world. For we are touching the body of Christ twenty-four hours. We have twenty-four hours in His presence, and so you and I. You too must try to bring that presence of God into

your family for the family that prays together stays together. And I think that we in our family we don't need bombs and guns, to destroy or to bring peace—just get together, love one another, bring that peace, that joy, that strength of presence of each other in the home, and we will be able to overcome all the evil that is in the world....It is to God Almighty—how much we do does not matter, because He is infinite, but how much love we put in that action. How much we do to Him in the person that we are serving.

Let us keep that joy of loving Jesus in our hearts, and share that joy with all we come in touch with. That radiating joy is real, for we have no reason not to be happy because we have Christ with us. Christ in our hearts, Christ in the poor we meet, Christ in the smile that we give and the smile we receive. Let us make that one point that no child will be unwanted, and also that we meet each other always with a smile, especially when it is difficult to smile.

To be able to do this, our Sisters, our lives have to be woven with prayer. They have to be woven with Christ to be able to understand, to be able to share. Today there is so much suffering and I feel that passion of Christ is being relived all over again. Are we there to share that passion, to share that suffering of people—around the world, not only in the poor countries.

An Interview

When times come when we can't pray, it is very simple: if Jesus is in my heart let Him pray, let me allow Him to pray in me, to talk to His Father in the silence of my heart. Since I cannot speak—He will speak; since I cannot pray He will pray. That's why often we should say: "Jesus in my heart I believe in your faithful love for me, I love you." And when we have nothing to give—let us give Him that nothingness. When we cannot pray—let us give that inability to Him.

For us who have the precious gift of Holy Communion every day, that contact with Christ is our prayer; that love for Christ, that joy in His presence, that surrender to His love is our prayer. For prayer is nothing but that complete surrender, complete oneness with Christ. And this is what makes us contemplatives in the heart of the world.

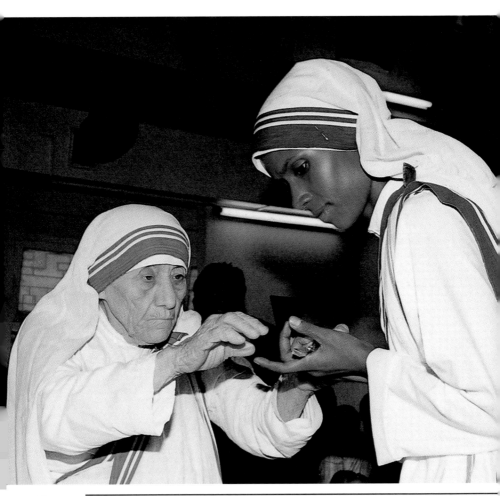

Letters from Mother's Last Years

God cannot fill what is full—He can fill only emptiness—deep poverty—and your "yes" is the beginning of being or becoming empty. It is not how much we really have to give but how empty we are—so that we can receive fully in our life and let Him live His life in us. In you today—He wants to relive His complete submission to His Father—allow Him to do so. It does not matter what you feel but what He feels in you. Take away your eyes from yourself and rejoice that you have nothing—that you are nothing—that you can do nothing.

*Give Jesus a big smile—each time your nothing-
ness frightens you. This is the poverty of Jesus.
You and I must let Him live in us and through
us in the world. Cling to Our Lady for she
too—before she could become full of the grace
of Jesus—had to go through that darkness.
"How could this be done..." but the moment
she said "yes" she had need to go in haste and
give Jesus to John and his family. Keep giving
Jesus to your people not by words—but by
radiating His holiness and spreading His
fragrance of love everywhere you go.*

Just keep the joy of Jesus as your strength—be happy and at peace, accept whatever He gives—and give whatever He takes with a big smile. You belong to Him—tell Him—I am yours—and if you cut me to pieces every single piece will be only all yours.

God longs to share His holiness with us: "Be holy for I am holy." We must long to receive it, and this longing is prayer. Let us love to pray, often feel the need for prayer, take the trouble to pray, for prayer enlarges the heart until it is capable of containing God's gift of Himself—His holiness. Ask, seek, and your heart will grow big enough to receive Him and keep Him as your own.

Lent is a time of preparation for Easter. But Easter comes only after the pain, suffering and death of Holy Thursday and Good Friday. That is exactly like our life. We look forward to rising with Jesus, but each one of us must go through pain, sorrow, suffering, sickness and death. Because of the promise of the Resurrection, we do not have to be afraid. We can accept all suffering as a gift of God. We may shed a few tears, but inside we will be at peace, and have a deep sense of joy.

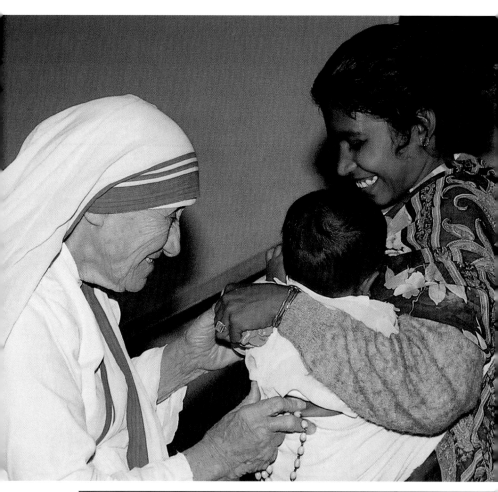

Instead of death and sorrow, let us bring peace and joy to the world. To do this we must beg God for His gift of peace and learn to love and accept each other as brothers and sisters, children of God. We know that the best place for children to learn how to love and to pray is in the family by seeing the love and prayer of their mother and father....when families are strong and united, children can see God's special love in the love of their father and mother and can grow to make their country a loving prayerful place.

On my "business card," it is written,

The fruit of silence is prayer

The fruit of prayer is faith

The fruit of faith is love

The fruit of love is service

The fruit of service is peace

This is very good "business"! And it makes the people think. Some of them hold it in their hands and read it over and over again. Sometimes, they ask me to explain it. But you see, everything begins with prayer that is born of our hearts.

The Last Letter

This brings you Mother's love, prayer and blessing that each one of you may be only all for Jesus through Mary. I know that Mother says often—"Be only all for Jesus through Mary"—but that is because that is all Mother wants for you, all Mother wants from you. If in your heart you are only all for Jesus through Mary and if you do everything only all for Jesus through Mary you will be true Missionaries of Charity.

We have much to thank God for, especially that he has given us Our Lady's spirit to be the spirit of our Society. Loving trust and total surrender made Our Lady say "Yes" to the message of the angel, and cheerfulness made her run in haste to serve her cousin Elizabeth. That is so much our life—saying "Yes" to Jesus and running in haste to serve Him in the poorest of the poor. Let us keep very close to Our Lady and she will make that same spirit grow in each one of us.

September 10th is coming very close. That is another beautiful chance for us to stand near Our Lady to listen to the Thirst of Jesus and to answer with our whole heart. It is only with Our Lady that we can hear Jesus cry "I thirst," and it is only with Our Lady that we can thank God properly for giving this great gift to our Society.

Now I have heard that Jesus is giving us one more gift. This year, one hundred years after she went home to Jesus, Holy Father is declaring the Little Flower to be a Doctor of

the Church. Can you imagine—for doing little things with great love the Church is making her a Doctor, like St. Augustine and the big St. Teresa! It is just like Jesus said in the Gospel to the one who was seated in the lowest place, "Friend, come up higher."

So let us keep very small and follow the Little Flower's way of trust and love and joy, and we will fulfill Mother's promise to give saints to Mother Church.

Afterword

Mother Teresa passed away on September 5, 1997. She was eighty-seven years old at that time. The documents in this book are collected from her letters to her coworkers (supporters of Mother) written in her last years, her famous speeches and so on. She used to write letters to her sisters and coworkers, starting with the words "My Dear Children." These letters are still read among many people as her last messages.

Before joining the Society of Jesus, I was working as a volunteer with Mother Teresa for about a year, from 1994 to 1995, in Calcutta. Though Mother did not like to be photographed, she permitted it on special occasions for the sake of her sisters and their families. The pictures in this book were taken, basically, on these occasions. Up to now I have shared these pictures only with her sisters and

my friends to remember Mother. But recently I

received a letter from Sister Nirmala, who is a

successor of Mother, which states that she

would permit the pictures to be published for

"the glory of God and good of men." So I

decided to publish this book hoping that Jesus'

Gospel will become familiar to many people

through Mother. Actually Mother was a person

like a mirror reflecting the existence of Jesus. It

is sure everybody who met her felt that Jesus

loved them through her.

I pray that readers of this book may meet with Jesus, who will never abandon us, through Mother Teresa.

March 16, 2001
Hiroshi Katayanagi, S.J.

Sources and Notes

pp. 7 to 19: A letter written in Varanasi, a holy place for Hindus. Mother Teresa made mention of her death in this letter.

pp. 20 to 23: Navin Chawla, Mother Teresa: The Authorized Biography *(New York: Penguin Books, 1998).*

pp. 24 to 35: A speech made at the Nobel Peace Prize reception on December 10, 1979.

pp. 36 to 39: Eileen Egan, "Such a Vision of the Street" (New York: Doubleday Image, 1985).

pp. 40 to 45: To a priest.

pp. 46 to 47: To coworkers, December 28, 1993.

pp. 48 to 49: To coworkers, Lent 1996.

pp. 50 to 51: To coworkers, Christmas 1995.

pp. 52 to 53: To coworkers, Lent 1996.

pp. 54 to 61: To everybody, September 5, 1997.
   This letter was called Mother's last message by her sisters.
   It was written on her very last day.

Picture Captions

Caseside: May 1995, at St. Mary's Church in Calcutta, before final vows.

p. iv: A door of the Motherhouse of the Missionaries of Charity.

p. 2: November 27, 1995, at a courtyard of the Motherhouse. Mother is talking to the sisters who took their final vows.

p. 4: November 20, 1994, on the grounds of St. Xavier College.

p. 6: December 8, 1994, at a chapel in the Motherhouse. Mother is blessing the sisters who took their first vows.

p. 8: May 10, 1994, at St. Mary's Church in Calcutta, before final vows.

p. 10: A cross at the Motherhouse.

p. 12: May 24, 1997, at a convent in Rome. Three months later she died in Calcutta.

p. 14: October 22, 1995, Mass at a chapel of the Motherhouse.

p. 16: January 6, 1995, at a courtyard of the Motherhouse, on the anniversary of Mother's arrival in India.

p. 18: December 7, 1994, at St. Mary's Church in Calcutta, before final vows. Sister Agnes is on Mother's right side.

p. 20: January 6, 1995, at a courtyard of the Motherhouse, on the anniversary of Mother's arrival in India.

p. 22: December 7, 1994, at St. Mary's Church in Calcutta, before final vows.

p. 24: October 21, 1995, at an ordination.

p. 26: August 22,1995, at a home for the sick and dying destitute in Calcutta.

p. 28: August 22, 1995, at a home for the sick and dying destitute in Calcutta.

p. 30: August 22, 1995, at a home for the sick and dying destitute in Calcutta.

p. 32: January 6, 1995, at a courtyard of the Motherhouse, on the anniversary of Mother's arrival in India.

p. 34: At a courtyard of the Motherhouse.

p. 36: October 21, 1995, after an ordination.

p. 38: December 7, 1994, at St. Mary's Church in Calcutta, before final vows.

p. 40: May 19, 1995, at St. Mary's Church in Calcutta. Mother is passing a cross to a sister who took her first vows.

p. 42: December 7, 1994, at St. Mary's Church in Calcutta, before final vows.

p. 44: November 27, 1995, at St. Mary's Church in Calcutta, before final vows.

p. 46: October 22, 1995, at a chapel of the Motherhouse.

p. 48: August 26, 1995, at a courtyard of the Motherhouse, on her eighty-fifth birthday.

p. 50: December 7, 1994, at St. Mary's Church in Calcutta, before final vows.

p. 52: August 26, 1995, at a courtyard of the Motherhouse, on her eighty-fifth birthday.

p. 54: December 8, 1994, at a chapel of the Motherhouse. The sisters who took their first vows.

p. 56: December 7, 1994, at St. Mary's Church in Calcutta, before final vows.

p. 58: May 19, 1995, at St. Mary's Church in Calcutta, before first vows.

p. 60: May 19, 1995, at St. Mary's Church in Calcutta, before first vows.

Hiroshi Katayanagi, S.J., is a Jesuit scholastic. He was born at Saitama prefecture, Japan, in 1971. In 1994 he graduated from Keio University in Tokyo. From 1994 to 1995 he worked in Calcutta as a volunteer of Mother Teresa. In 1998 he entered the Society of Jesus.

Of Related Interest

Family Prayers

by Nick Aiken and Rowan Williams

Many families today are looking for guidance on how to bring their faith into the routine of home and working life. This heartening collection of prayers touches on a wide range of everyday matters. There are prayers to say at meal times, at the end of the day, or on special occasions, such as a birthday or Christmas. There are prayers for particular situations, such as when someone we love is ill, when a child is unhappy at school or when we want to say we are sorry.

Many of the prayers are casual and conversational in tone. Some of these have been contributed by school children while others, more formal in style, have been especially written by Rowan Williams.

Hardcover, 0550-0, 64 pages, $14.95
Color photographs and illustrations throughout
Available from Paulist Press
www.paulistpress.com
Phone (800) 218-1903 Fax (800) 836-3161

Great Spirits 1000—2000

The Fifty-two Christians Who Most Influenced
Their Millennium

Edited by Selina O'Grady and John Wilkins

Foreword by Kathleen Norris

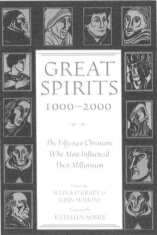

Today's best thinkers write about history's best thinkers in this rich and incisive volume. From Anselm of Canterbury to Pope John Paul II, the most influential Christian mystics, reformers, theologians, and church leaders are profiled by contemporary superstars. Contibutors include: Robert Ellsberg, Lawrence Cunningham, Eamon Duffy, Rowan Williams, and many, many more.

Hardcover, 0546-2, 224 pages, $16.95
Available from Paulist Press
www.paulistpress.com
Phone (800) 218-1903 Fax (800) 836-3161